Coping with

MULTIPLE SCLEROSIS

Betty Burnett and Rob Gevertz

The Rosen Publishing Group, Inc.
New York

Published in 2001 by The Rosen Publishing Group, Inc.
29 East 21st Street, New York, NY 10010

Cover photo by Antonio Mari

Library of Congress Cataloging-in-Publication Data

Burnett, Betty, 1940–
Coping with multiple sclerosis / Betty Burnett and Rob Gevertz. — 1st ed.
p. cm. — (Coping)
Includes bibliographical references and index.
ISBN 0-8239-3204-4 (library binding)
1. Multiple sclerosis — Juvenile literature. [1. Multiple sclerosis.]
[DNLM: 1. Multiple Sclerosis — Popular Works.
WL 360 B964c 2001] I. Gevertz, Rob. II. Title. III. Series.
RC377 .B865 2001
616.8'34—dc21
                                                                00-012606

Manufactured in the United States of America

About the Authors

Betty Burnett, Ph.D., is originally from Hartford, Connecticut, and is the author of more than a dozen books. After stops in Kansas City, St. Louis, Chicago, Dallas, and Tucson, she currently lives in El Paso, Texas. She is on the road as much as possible, finding new information to write about.

Rob Gevertz, a native of El Paso, Texas, lives and writes in that border town. He shares his computer with his wonderful wife, Lee Ann, and three great children, who are all a big support in his fight against MS. You can also find him exercising, teaching, and playing trombone.

Contents

Introduction:
I Can't Have MS!

Kelly wiped the sweat from her eyes. What was the matter? Why couldn't she focus? This was the make-or-break game, the one that would decide if she was going to be on the tennis team or not. She needed to see straight. The ball lobbed toward her, and she lunged toward it. Her racket missed it by a foot.

"Heads up, Kelly!" called her partner.

Kelly shook her head. What was happening? She felt rubbery, not clear and sharp like she usually did. Usually, that is, until lately, when this blurriness had caught hold of her. Suddenly she stumbled and fell. She had tripped over her own feet.

She struggled to stand up, but before she could, the coach was beside her. He hunkered down, his face concerned.

"What's the matter, Kelly?"

Tears stung her eyes. "I guess I didn't make the team," she said.

He shrugged. "I'm concerned about you. You're not moving like you used to. Do you feel okay?"

"I feel fine!" Kelly almost shouted. Was it obvious to everyone that she was turning into a klutz? She

forced herself to stand up, her face blazing. "What are you staring at?" she called to her partner. She wanted to throw her racket straight at the net, but she wasn't sure she could hit it. *I'm not going to cry,* she told herself. *I'll just walk straight out of here like I couldn't care less.*

But she felt wobbly again and automatically reached out, catching the coach's arm.

"Take it easy, girl," he said. "Let's sit you down in the shade. You might have sunstroke."

Kelly felt an immediate sense of relief. *Of course! Sunstroke! That could happen to anyone.* Then her heart sank. *It wasn't sunstroke the other night, when she bumped into the wall.*

She jammed her racket into her gym bag. "No, I'll just go home. Take an aspirin."

The coach nodded. "Get some rest, too. You look tired. Maybe you ought to stop by the student health center and get checked out."

So I look tired, Kelly thought as she started the short walk to her apartment. *Well, who wouldn't? I'm only taking sixteen hours this semester, working ten hours at the library, and practicing tennis every spare minute. Who has time to wait in line at the health center? Besides, I'm not sick.*

The block in front of her stretched out like it was a mile. She was conscious of each step she took. She was so tired it was an effort to keep moving forward. She felt as if she were walking through Jell-O. And here came the blurriness again. She blinked and shook her head.

I'll go to the health center now, she decided. *I've got to know what's wrong.*

2

Dr. Garfield was more like somebody's grand-mother than a doctor. For the first few minutes after Kelly blurted out her symptoms, she just chatted, as if nothing was wrong.

"What are your career plans, Kelly?"

"I want to be a geologist. I love rocks." Kelly laughed self-consciously. People thought she was nuts the way she collected rocks.

Finally they got around to the health questions. She was nineteen years old. Not overweight. Her parents were both still alive and in good health. No, she didn't smoke. Didn't drink much, just a beer or two on Friday nights. No recreational drugs. She exercised and stayed away from junk food as much as she could. Got along well with her roommates and her family. Was doing well in school.

Dr. Garfield asked her to walk down the hall, being careful to stay in the center of the linoleum squares. Kelly went up and down the hall twice, concentrating on walking in a straight line. She thought she had passed the test and began to feel optimistic.

"Let's go in my office and talk," Dr. Garfield said.

Kelly sat across the desk from Dr. Garfield and waited.

"I'm going to order some tests for you, but we can't do them here. You'll have to go to St. Matthew's Medical Center."

"Why?"

"There are some indications that you could have MS," Dr. Garfield said.

"MS?"

"Multiple sclerosis."

Kelly felt as if she'd been blindsided.

The vision of a wheelchair popped into her mind. She was wearing a bib and someone was spooning

3

applesauce into her mouth. Her stomach turned and she was afraid she was going to be sick.

"Kelly," the doctor was saying. "Take a deep breath. I said 'some indications.' That is not a certainty, and I told you that much only because you're a sensible, intelligent woman. Now don't get hysterical on me."

Kelly couldn't trust her voice. Her mind was swirling. Words didn't make sense. She rose unsteadily.

Dr. Garfield put her hand on Kelly's shoulder and looked into her eyes. "Kelly, if you have MS, I want you to know: You can cope. Do you hear me? You can cope with it."

Kelly nodded, but she did not feel that she could cope with anything right now. She started out the door, then turned back.

"No, Dr. Garfield, I don't have MS. I'm healthy. I know I'm healthy. I feel fine. I can't have MS!"

Twenty-five years ago, the diagnosis of MS meant you were headed for a wheelchair. Today, it rarely does, and certainly not full-time. Tomorrow, the disease may be only a slight annoyance.

MS is a disease that is linked to the immune system in ways that are still not clear. It affects the nervous system and muscular control. To understand MS, these systems must be understood as well. It helps, too, to know what MS is not.

Even in its mildest form, MS is life-changing. But it's not necessarily life-worsening. MS veterans emphasize that a positive attitude is the most important element in coping with this unpredictable and frustrating disease. But there are many other available forms of aid: various kinds of medical treatment, psychological support, and practical advice for self-help.

The long-term outlook today for a young person diagnosed with MS is bright. There is no reason, for instance, why Kelly cannot pursue her dream of becoming a field geologist, even if she decides she wants to work in Tierra del Fuego. Marriage, parenthood, travel, and exciting careers are all in the picture for young people with MS. That doesn't mean that there won't be bad days, even weeks, or that everything will follow exactly according to plan—but it never does anyway.

What it does mean is that MS is a disease that can be coped with. It will not overwhelm someone with determination and optimism. Knowing the facts about MS is a major part of the coping strategy.

What Is Multiple Sclerosis?

Multiple sclerosis (MS) is a disease of the nervous system that affects the muscles. It causes muscles to weaken, twitch, or clench without voluntary control. It also affects vision and sensation (how the skin feels).

MS is a chronic, lifelong disease. It may get better, but it never goes away. It may be totally disabling, or it may be just an irritation. Most cases fall somewhere between the two extremes.

The most frustrating thing about MS is that it is unpredictable. Some symptoms are clear; many are not—and symptoms come and go. When they are in remission, life is almost normal. Then a "flare" or "attack" can bring the symptoms back. An attack may have a definite cause, such as too much stress, or it may occur with no warning and for no reason.

During an MS attack, the white matter (myelin) of the central nervous system becomes inflamed. These inflammations leave lesions on the brain and spinal cord, which become covered with scar tissue called sclerosis. Because there are many such lesions, the disease is called multiple sclerosis.

Researchers today are considering the possibility that MS is not a specific disease at all, but a syndrome—a group of similar diseases triggered by different causes and all resulting in myelin destruction—because the symptoms, pathology, and responses to treatment vary so widely. Most diseases are more easily identifiable, have a more clearly defined course, and respond in specific ways to treatment. MS is a mystery.

Is MS a New Disease?

The disease was first diagnosed in 1849, but there are descriptions of an MS-like disease from as early as the fourteenth century. It seems that there are more cases now than earlier in our history, but that may be because there are better diagnostic techniques today. Also, disabled people are more visible today—they no longer have to stay at home, inactive and alone.

Who Gets MS?

There is a definite pattern to those who get MS, which makes the disease even more puzzling.

Age
The great majority of cases occur in adults between the ages of twenty and forty. Children under age fifteen—as young as seven—and adults over age sixty have developed the disease, but only in rare cases. Apparently, the brain must be in a certain stage of growth for the disease to get a foothold.

Gender
Women are almost twice as likely as men to be affected. The onset of the disease appears earlier in women than it does in men.

7

Race

MS is almost exclusively a "white" disease. People of other races who contract MS usually, if not always, have a Caucasian ancestor somewhere down the line.

Environment

The only environmental factor that remains constant is weather. People in temperate climates, such as found in the United States, Canada, and most of Europe, get MS; people in tropical climates, such as in Central America and Africa, do not. Someone who moves from a temperate climate to a tropical one after age fifteen is as much at risk as if he or she had not moved. Scientists have not been able to draw any conclusions from this observation, however.

The one environmental factor that affects almost all people with MS is heat: High external temperature, fever, or strenuous activities make symptoms worse.

Periodically, reports of MS "clusters" appear, which makes it seem as if there could be an epidemic. None of these epidemics has been traced to environmental factors (or to any other causes). Other neurological diseases—Parkinson's disease or Minamata disease, for instance—have been linked to a concentration of heavy metals in the environment, but MS has not.

Incidence of MS

About 200 new cases of MS are diagnosed in the United States each week. More than one-quarter of a million Americans now have symptoms of the disease. It is the second most common neurological cause of disability in young adults, after head or spinal cord injury. It may be that many more people have MS lesions than are counted because they do not show symptoms or they have such mild symptoms that they do not seek medical help.

What Causes MS?

So far, no one knows what causes MS. It is believed to be an autoimmune disease (one in which the body attacks its own tissues). But why does MS happen? Is it triggered by a virus or other infectious agent? Is it caused by a combination of factors? Scientists think these questions will be answered within the next ten years. The immune system is discussed in chapter 3.

Genetics may play a role in determining a person's susceptibility to MS. Some populations, such as Aleuts or Bantus, never get MS.

In the population at large, the chance of developing MS is less than a tenth of 1 percent. However, for a first-degree family member of someone with MS (children and siblings), the percentage rises to 3 percent. For identical twins, the likelihood that the second twin will develop MS after the first twin does is about thirty percent.

An intriguing possibility is that MS may be associated with the HLA (human leukocyte antigen) complex, which is a series of genes on chromosome 6. These genes are present in certain other diseases, such as arthritis and inflammatory bowel disease.

What Are the Symptoms?

The general symptoms of MS are fatigue, blurring vision, some loss of coordination, numbness and tingling, and muscle weakness. Kelly had difficulty focusing and felt awkward and clumsy, which is very disturbing to an athlete. Sometimes she ran into walls or staggered slightly, making her roommates accuse her of drinking on the sly. But each instance is unique.

> *Roger was twenty-six with a new MBA, a new job, and a new wife when he started to feel the urge to urinate every hour and then even more frequently. He often had to leave a meeting and hurry down the hall to the men's room. His coworkers were irritated with the interruptions, and he was embarrassed by causing them. One night at a basketball game, he missed most of the action because he spent so much time going to and from the rest room. He decided to schedule an appointment with his doctor. It turns out he had also been experiencing some on-and-off double vision, but he never put the symptoms together.*

> *Cynthia, a pharmacist, was thirty-five when she began to notice problems. Her vision was fine, but she had trouble concentrating on her work and she frequently forgot if she'd filled a prescription or not. She knew she could endanger others—much as an airline pilot or surgeon with the same symptoms could—and didn't waste time getting a checkup. She also felt a mysterious stab of pain in her face now and then—trigeminal neuralgia—and the sensation of electricity running up and down her backbone when she turned her head suddenly.*

Many MS symptoms are subjective, which means that they are not necessarily noticeable to anyone but you. These must be reported by the patient. But some symptoms are objective, or clinical, and can be measured by a physician.

Clinical Symptoms of MS

Spasticity
The continuous contraction of a muscle. This contraction causes stiffness or tightness of the muscles and may interfere with gait, movement, and speech. It is usually caused by damage to the portion of the brain or spinal cord that controls voluntary movement. It is seen in MS, cerebral palsy, brain trauma, or head injury.

Myoclonus
An involuntary twitch of a muscle or group of muscles. Everyone is familiar with some form of myoclonus—hiccupping or jerking awake just before falling into a deep sleep, for instance. Sometimes after prolonged stress—a bicycle marathon or long race—muscles will twitch for a few moments before they can relax. Myoclonus frequently occurs in MS, Parkinson's disease, and Alzheimer's disease.

Ataxia
The inability to maintain balance while walking. A characteristic reeling gait with poorly coordinated movements, it is commonly seen in intoxicated people.

Paresthesia
A "pins and needles" feeling or a spontaneously occurring sensation of burning, creeping, or prickling on the skin that has no apparent cause.

Are There Different Kinds of MS?

There are three generally recognized types of MS, which are classified according to the pattern of disease activity. The mildest form, and the most common by far, is relapsing-remitting (R/R). Patients have flare-ups of the disease, lasting for days, weeks, or months, followed by a nearly complete recovery. The disease usually does not progress between flares.

The secondary-progressive form (S/P) of the disease is marked by progressive weakness between flares. This frequently is seen as the patient ages. About 10 percent of patients have a steadily worsening form of MS without any remission. This type is called primary-progressive (P/P).

How Is the Diagnosis Made?

MS can be difficult to diagnose because there is no single laboratory test that clearly identifies the disease. It is primarily diagnosed through a neurological exam that tests for abnormal reflexes, muscle weakness or lack of coordination, changes in the degree or kind of sensation, and damage to the optic nerve.

MRI (magnetic resonance imaging) can reveal the characteristic patches, or lesions, in the brain. Absence of lesions does not rule out the disease. A spinal tap can be performed to examine the spinal fluid for elevated levels of certain immune system proteins that are frequently present in people with MS. And the evoked potential test is given to determine how long it takes an electrical nerve impulse, such as that generated by a flashing light, to travel through nerve fibers to the brain.

After Kelly checked herself into St. Matthew's Medical Center, Dr. Garfield ordered so many tests that Kelly wondered if MS was fatal. She was glad her parents had come to lend moral support and help calm her fears.

First she was given the evoked potentials because her vision was obviously causing her problems. The technician clicked a clicker, then a machine wired to Kelly recorded the time it took her body to respond to the sound. Next came an EMG (electromyogram). For this test, technicians marked Kelly's legs and placed electrodes on them. Then Dr. Monroe, the neurologist, stuck a needle (connected to a machine by an electrical wire) into various locations on her legs. It was very uncomfortable. She was asked to move her muscles to test nerve function.

As if that wasn't enough, the neurologist shocked her legs to test the response in her nerves. Finally, Kelly was taken for an MRI of her brain and of her spinal column. This wasn't painful, but she felt anxious to be so confined, even for such a short time. As soon as the technician ordered her not to move, she could feel a thousand itches that begged to be scratched. The noise inside the cylinder surprised her—it was the sound of the magnetism of her own body.

The next day, Dr. Garfield and Dr. Monroe entered Kelly's room. They didn't look either joyful or sad, so Kelly couldn't guess what they'd say. After a few minutes of small talk, she asked about the results of the tests.

Dr. Garfield looked straight into her eyes and said, "Kelly, you have multiple sclerosis." Before Kelly could react, she continued, "Don't think the worst and don't panic. You're down, but far from out."

13

The words echoed in her mind: "Down, but far from out."

Dr. Monroe said, "Kelly, we are going to start IV steroids on you immediately. You will more than likely begin to respond in a day or two. We have a whole arsenal of treatments at our disposal. If you don't respond to one treatment, we have others. There are several side effects to steroids, but none that are long-lasting as long as the regimen is well managed."

Kelly nodded, not trusting her voice. The doctor went on: "After you feel better, you will enter physical therapy to regain some or all of your strength, coordination, and balance. MS is unpredictable. This may be your only attack, or you may have attacks once in a while. Very few cases of MS are severe. Fortunately, we have some pharmaceuticals available that will minimize the severity of your case. You will have to learn to manage your life. There is no cure for MS at this time, but, like diabetes, it is manageable. Researchers are making new discoveries all the time.

"Just don't give up on yourself, not now. You must try, push, and persevere. If you feel like you're drowning in despair, let us know. We can help. A little depression is normal. A lot is damaging. Do you have any questions?"

Kelly could not digest everything Dr. Monroe had said. She asked only, "Will I ever be normal again?"

"I don't know, Kelly. The hope is that you have a light case. Each one is different. Much, but not all, of your recovery and progression through life is up to you. I've heard some of my better patients say things like 'I have MS, but it doesn't have me.' I'd wonder

about you if you weren't scared and angry right now. Just know I'm here to help you. Call me when you need me, day or night."

The most important question that most newly diagnosed MS patients have is the one that has no clear answer.

What Is the Course of the Disease?

The course of the disease differs with each patient and depends on many factors. Some are under a patient's control, others are not. In general, the outlook is good and today's intensive research may lead to more effective treatment very soon.

Some of the factors that influence how successfully a person with MS copes with the disease are:

- ➯ The support of friends, family, and a first-rate health care system

- ➯ A positive, realistic attitude and the ability to roll with the punches

- ➯ A willingness to learn how to manage the symptoms

- ➯ The ability to make common sense decisions regarding health and safety

The life expectancy for most people with MS today is the same as it is for people the same age who don't have MS. Life goals, including career and family, may have to be modified but can be achieved.

The Nervous System

According to the National Multiple Sclerosis Society, the key to coping with MS is learning everything possible about both health and the disease. They offer a program called Knowledge Is Power that encourages patients to participate in their own treatment by being able to make informed decisions.

The best place to start learning is with the nervous system. It's the job of the nervous system to run things. It collects information at one spot and sends it to another for interpretation and action. The senses are the information collectors; the brain makes sense of the data they collect and issues orders; the muscles act on those orders.

Receptors in the eyes, ears, nose, skin, and muscles register data and send it to the brain for processing. The cerebral cortex of the brain interprets the messages and sends directions to the midbrain, which relays them to the brain stem and the spinal cord. All along the way, via electrochemical impulses, nerves convey these messages to muscles and glands, which do—usually—what they're programmed to do.

This whole process—transmission of information, the interpretation and decision making, and the resulting action—takes only a nanosecond.

16

Say you're driving in heavy traffic on a freeway and someone cuts in front of you. What are you going to do— swerve, brake, honk? Whatever you do depends on your reaction time (how quickly your body responds to the stimulus). Eye to rearview mirror, foot to brake, hand to horn.

Well-trained drivers don't have to think about what to do. They do it automatically. And that's the way we live most of our lives, on automatic pilot.

But any sort of neurological impairment or disorder interrupts the smooth flow of this process. Instead of responding automatically to a stimulus, the nervous system behaves as if there's a loose wire. The confused body responds slowly, inappropriately, or not at all. (These disorders are discussed more fully in chapter 4.)

The nervous system is actually two systems: the central nervous system (CNS), made up of the brain and spinal cord, and the peripheral nervous system, which includes the nerves in all the other parts of the body.

The CNS

If we could get inside our own heads to take a tour of the CNS, we'd start at the top: the brain. The brain is protected by the skull and is enclosed in three membranes called meninges. (The disease meningitis is simply inflammation of the meninges, just as tonsillitis is inflammation of the tonsils.) Cerebrospinal fluid circulates between the two innermost layers, which further protect the delicate neural tissues of the brain.

There are three parts of the brain: the forebrain, midbrain, and hindbrain. The forebrain is the manager of the operation. It is mainly composed of the cerebrum—what we usually mean when we say "brain." The cerebrum consists of two hemispheres, which almost completely fill the skull. They are partially separated from each other by a deep median cleft, the longitudinal cerebral fissure.

The right hemisphere, which controls the left side of the body, seems to be involved in spatial perception and is important in the development of art, fantasy, and poetry. The left hemisphere, which controls the right side of the body, plays a greater role in more concrete skills, such as mathematics and logic. The two hemispheres are connected by the corpus callosum. When this bridge is destroyed in a head injury or by some other means, the "left hand doesn't know what the right hand is doing."

The outer layer of nerve cells, covering the surface of the cerebral hemispheres in deep folds, is the cerebral cortex. This is the so-called gray matter.

Cognition—the act of acquiring knowledge—occurs in the cerebral cortex. We learn through the comprehension and use of speech, visual perception, and making calculations. To learn anything we have to be able to pay attention, process information, recall events, plan for the future, and solve problems. All these functions are high-level jobs and add up to something we call intelligence.

The gray matter is also the area responsible for self-consciousness (being aware of who and where we are) and refined feelings, such as affection or remorse. The so-called primitive emotions—rage and fear, for instance—are lodged in the limbic system or midbrain. The cerebrum directs voluntary and precise muscle action, such as threading a needle or changing a carburetor. The most serious disease affecting the cerebral cortex is

Alzheimer's, which gradually destroys all its functions, beginning with memory.

The cerebellum makes up the midbrain and is located just above the brain stem. It is chiefly responsible for controlling balance and coordinating movements, including the speed of speech and eye movement. It has no ability to learn. It is the cerebellum that is most frequently disturbed in neuromuscular disability.

The brain stem or hindbrain is the portion of the brain that connects with the spinal cord. It consists mainly of the medulla oblongata, which is crucial for maintaining life. Because the medulla controls respiration, heartbeat, and blood pressure, brain stem injuries are almost always fatal.

Most of the cranial nerves—the ones going to and from the head—enter or exit the brain through the brain stem. The brain stem leads to the spinal cord, the main nerve trunk, which is enclosed and protected by the vertebrae of the backbone. Efferent nerves branch off from the spinal cord and go to various organs and muscles. Partner afferent nerves return from organs and muscles to the spinal cord. This network of nerves is called the peripheral nervous system.

The Peripheral Nervous System

The peripheral nervous system is divided into the voluntary system and autonomic (involuntary) system. The autonomic system controls the internal organs and glands, the heart rate, and such functions as the production of sweat. It is composed of the sympathetic and parasympathetic systems, which have almost opposite functions. The sympathetic system responds to stress by preparing the body for action—increasing the heart rate and blood pressure, for instance. The parasympathetic system slows the heart rate, decreases blood pressure, and stimulates the digestive system. These functions are normally outside of conscious control, although biofeed-back, deep meditation, and yoga techniques can control them somewhat.

The voluntary nervous system connects to skeletal muscles, the muscles that move the bones. These nerves and muscles are activated by choice and design. Do you want to change a channel, punch in a phone number, click on an icon? Just tell your fingers what to do. Once they know the drill, the activity becomes automatic, but not as automatic as breathing or digesting dinner. You still have to make conscious decisions about which channel, which number, which icon you want.

At the cellular level, each nerve is made of neurons. Each of these billions of neurons may have thousands of branches that connect it to other neurons. Neurons communicate by way of neurotransmitters, chemicals that act as messengers bringing information to and from receptors. Neurotransmitters in your eyes will register a complaint if the sun is too bright for them to be comfortable. This makes you reach for sunglasses or step into the shade.

Glia cells are the housekeepers of the nervous system. They clean up dead cells, transport nutrients to neurons, and hold neurons in place. Two types of glia cells are important in MS, oligodendroglia and Schwann cells.

Myelin

The nerves in both the central nervous system and the peripheral nervous system are protected by a sheath of myelin (white matter), a fatty substance that insulates them, much as insulators protect electric wires. Oligodendroglia manufacture myelin in the central nervous system and Schwann cells provide myelin in the peripheral nervous system.

This myelin is the target of MS. During an MS episode or attack, certain unpredictable sites on the myelin sheath become inflamed.

Recurring inflammation damages myelin. The patchy areas of inflammation and demyelination typical of MS are called plaques. Plaques disrupt or block nerve signals that would normally pass through with the speed of light. Wherever they occur, they result in a breakdown in communication. The brain says, "I want to click on this icon." The nerves send the message to the spinal cord and through the efferent nerves to the hand, but somewhere along the route is a tiny bit of plaque that stalls or reroutes the request. The hand gets a faulty message and what should be a simple click becomes a major production.

Plaques—or demyelination anywhere in the CNS—affect the function of nerves and muscles and result in unstable gait or uncoordinated fingers. Another common result is anesthesia, the loss of feeling (pain and touch sensation) over part or all of the body, or paresthesia, the feeling of being pricked with a thousand pins and needles.

Blood-Brain Barrier

Another factor in the development of MS is the blood-brain barrier. The blood-brain barrier is a semipermeable cell layer in the blood vessels in the central nervous system. If blue dye is injected into a person's bloodstream, all tissues turn blue—except the spinal cord and the brain. These two areas have their own blood circulatory system, which is separated from the main circulatory system by this barrier.

The blood-brain barrier prevents large molecules and potentially damaging substances and foreign organisms, such as viruses, from passing out of the regular blood stream into the brain and spinal cord. In this way it protects the brain from disease and contamination. It also maintains a stable environment for the brain, just as water in an indoor swimming pool can be kept at a constant level and temperature, without the uncertainties and possible contamination of a free-flowing stream.

A break in the blood-brain barrier somewhere along the spinal cord may underlie the disease process in MS. Such a break could allow pathogens to invade the CNS. If this can be proved, and the mechanism isolated, it will increase the likelihood of a cure for MS and perhaps for a program of prevention as well.

The blood-brain barrier is the interface between the nervous system and the immune system, and a disorder in the immune system is the second major component of MS.

The Immune System

Since the outbreak of AIDS in the early 1980s, the immune system has been a source of intense study. New findings appear weekly, and old ideas are constantly challenged. The idea behind the immune system is simple—repel all invaders—but the mechanisms are complex. Most of the time, the system works in our best interest and even saves our lives on occasion. But when it goes wrong, it can be a disaster.

The immune system protects the body from foreign substances. It develops during the first several years of a child's life. Infants are born from a safe, sterile environment into a world that is filled with risk. They are generally protected for the first few months of life by their mother's immunity. After that, they're on their own.

Viruses, bacteria, fungi, parasites, and toxins coat virtually everything we touch, eat, and breathe. People around us sneeze and cough. Germ-laden insects threaten us. Even the gentlest breeze is filled with pollen, dog dander, and the eggs of parasites.

Healthy children gradually build up a resistance to such perils, but not without getting sick once in a while, because it's sickness that produces the antigens that stimulate the immune system to produce antibodies that defeat disease.

No one is surprised when four-year-old Max comes home from day care with a cold. His runny nose, sore throat, and slight fever are his body's reactions to the presence of an antigen (literally something that is "against life"). If the antigen is a virus, there is little to do but wait it out until the symptoms subside. Max is totally unaware of the battle his immune system is waging against the virus, although it is as dramatic as the action videos he watches while he recovers.

The immune system must gear up and do battle each time a cold virus enters the system. At this point, it is impossible to be immune to colds, but it is possible, with the help of vitamins, lots of liquids, and rest, to fight them off. In twenty years or so, there may be one all-purpose vaccination for colds and flu.

If disease-causing bacteria, such as the ones that bring on strep throat, enter the system, the use of prescription antibiotics will shorten the disease time and severity. Some diseases are so overwhelming to the system that without today's immunizations, many of us would not have survived childhood. Before vaccination, smallpox killed hundreds of thousands of people each year. Only 100 years ago, diphtheria was the scourge of childhood, and fifty years ago, polio left thousands of children crippled.

Types of Immunity

The body offers two types of immunity: innate and adaptive (or acquired). Innate immunity is the first line of defense. It consists of the physical barriers to invasion: skin, tears, mucus, and saliva. Innate immunity also triggers the body's automatic response to injury, localized infection, or insect bites. The immediate redness, swelling, and itching that appear after a mosquito has had lunch at your expense are thanks to this system.

Innate immunity is a generalized response to danger. It cannot respond to individual diseases. Adaptive immunity, on the other hand, is tailor-made for disease control. It causes a specific reaction against a specific pathogen—the microorganism that causes a disease. Adaptive immunity has several unique characteristics:

⇝ It responds only after the invader is present, unlike tears and saliva, which are always present and do not change their chemistry in response to anything.

⇝ It has memory and responds better (faster and more powerfully) after the first exposure, even though the second exposure may be years later. Usually the reaction is so swift and thorough you may not know you've been infected. People who had chicken pox or mumps as children don't get them again, even though they may be exposed dozens of times.

⇝ It does not normally attack what it recognizes as its own body, only what it labels alien. When it does attack itself, it is because of a failure in the communication system.

The adaptive immune system operates at both the humoral (circulatory) and cellular levels. The avenue it travels is the lymphatic circulatory system. Lymph is a transparent fluid containing white blood cells—chiefly lymphocytes— approximately one trillion of them. Lymph circulates throughout the body, just as blood does.

Lymphocytes

Lymphocytes are small white blood cells that bear the major responsibility for carrying out activities of the immune system. They are formed and stored in lymph nodes, which dot the network in the armpit, groin, and neck and are noticeable only when they become infected and swollen. During childhood, the lymph tissue in tonsils and adenoids frequently becomes infected and these are often surgically removed. The spleen, an organ at the upper left of the abdomen, also produces and stores lymphocytes. There are two major classes of lymphocytes: B cells and T cells.

B Cells

B cells, which grow to maturity in the bone marrow, produce antibodies and mark antigens for destruction. One way antigens are destroyed is by macrophages, scavenger cells that actually ingest foreign antigens, just as the old Pac Man ate whatever got in his way.

T Cells

T cells mature in the thymus, behind the breastbone. Through their receptors, "helper" T cells recognize a specific antigen, say the one for strep *(Streptococcus pyogenes)*. Immediately they assist other cells to make antistrep antibodies, Y-shaped proteins called immunoglobulins. There are dozens of kinds of immunoglobulins. One kind binds to the strep bacteria at the ends of the arms of the Y, destroying them.

Other T cells, known as "killer" T's, attack diseased cells by bombarding them with lethal chemicals called cytokines. Cytokines control both the intensity and quality of the immune response. Because cytokines are so powerful, it's very important that killer T's know what they're doing and not use their power against good cells or cells that are minding their own business and have no disease-producing designs. Unfortunately, this doesn't always happen.

When an attack on antigens has been successfully won, still other T cells notify the armies of antibodies, macrophages, and killer T's of the victory and advise them to go home and get a good night's sleep. Not satisfied with that, they also instigate biochemical changes to suppress the immune system until the balance is back to normal and the number of circulating antibodies is decreased to "reserve" status. Unfortunately, this aspect of immunity doesn't always work either, and sometimes the immune system is suppressed longer than it should be, allowing pathogens to overrun the body.

Immune System Disorders

The most common immune system disorder is an allergic reaction. Practically everyone has at least one allergic reaction in his or her life. Pollen, cat dander, bee stings, and a thousand other airborne pollutants can cause a rapid allergic reaction by producing histamine, the chemical that brings about a runny nose, watery eyes, and sneezing. The sale of over-the-counter antihistamines goes up every spring and fall in response to the increased level of nature's bounty in the air.

A less common immune system disorder is the rejection of an organ transplant, even one from a close relative where the match is almost perfect. As transplants have become more common, drugs designed to avoid organ rejection have become more sophisticated. The use of synthetic body parts for transplants may introduce still more problems for the immune system.

Immune Deficiency

When the immune system does not respond as it should, with all flags waving and trumpets sounding, a deficiency is suspected. Some infants are born with a genetic deficiency and, unless they can live in a sterile environment, they die from the first infections they encounter.

Radiation used in the treatment of cancer weakens the immune system. Poor nutrition and environmental stress or fatigue also keep the immune system from operating at an optimum level, as anyone who has ever caught a cold during exam week knows.

The virus called HIV (human immunodeficiency virus) causes AIDS (acquired immunodeficiency syndrome) by infecting and eventually destroying T cells, and preventing the body from fighting off infection. People with AIDS have no resistance mechanisms to disease and are easy prey for pathogens.

Autoimmune Disease

When the body's defense system malfunctions and attacks a part of the body itself, rather than a foreign antigen, it produces an autoimmune disease. The list of these diseases is long and includes diabetes, lupus, rheumatoid arthritis, fibromyalgia, myasthenia gravis, and multiple sclerosis, among others. It is possible that autoimmune diseases will become more common as environmental pollutants become more toxic and confuse the body's defenses.

Although each autoimmune disease is different, they all share certain vague symptoms that are often not taken seriously: fatigue, occasional dizziness, and malaise—a feeling of not being well, but not quite being sick. Organs, tissues, and cells, such as those of red blood cells, blood vessels, endocrine glands, connective tissue, muscles, joints, and skin, can be affected by autoimmune diseases.

In the case of MS, several problems have been identified regarding the immune system. Apparently, T cells are unable to discriminate between good cells and harmful cells. They perceive friendly cells as enemies and attack them. Specifically, antimyelin T cells assault the myelin sheath on the nerves, destroying it in patches. This process is called demyelination. Macrophages are also involved in demyelination, although it's not clear how or why.

Researchers suspect that malfunctions in the blood-brain barrier allow components of the immune system to enter the central nervous system and cause damage, almost as if the gate on a school playground was left open and vandals poured in with baseball bats and tire irons, smashing whatever they could reach. Of course vandals can also climb over fences, ignoring gates, and this may also happen in the body.

Because so many scientists are working on the problem of autoimmunity, it probably won't be long before the malfunctioning mechanisms are identified. Only then can we start thinking about a cure for MS.

Other Neuromuscular Diseases and Disabilities

Several neuromuscular diseases and disabilities have symptoms similar to those of MS. They all involve a glitch somewhere in the connections between brain, nerves, and muscles. All of them require some sort of adaptation, and, fortunately, there are facilities, organizations, and help of various kinds for each.

It is easy for those who've had no experience with these diseases to confuse them. The following rundown may help answer questions about what MS isn't.

Muscular Dystrophy

Muscular dystrophy (MD) is frequently confused with MS because of the use of similar initials. MD, like MS, is a disease that causes weakness in the muscles. There are several types of MD. Because of the Labor Day telethons hosted by Jerry Lewis, the most familiar is the kind that affects children. There are also types of MD that affect adults—young, middle-aged, and elderly. MD is an inherited disease; it is not caused by a virus or by an injury. There is now no treatment for it except the use of physical therapy to tone the muscles.

Cerebral Palsy

Cerebral palsy (CP) is caused by a brain injury that occurs sometime between birth (or earlier) and two years of age. The injury can result from an accident or from a loss of oxygen to the brain. The most obvious signs of CP are spasticity (muscle rigidity) and myoclonus (involuntary twitching of muscles), and both are also seen in MS. It is not degenerative—it does not get worse, although there is some increased loss of mobility with aging—and it usually does not get better. The reasoning power of the brain is not damaged by CP, and it most often does not affect the senses. It frequently interferes with the muscles that control speech.

Occasionally, CP is part of multiple handicaps that appear in a child as a result of the mother having German measles while she was pregnant. In that case, the child may be blind, deaf, or developmentally disabled in addition to having CP.

Parkinson's Disease

Parkinson's disease rarely affects people under fifty-five. The actor Michael J. Fox, who was diagnosed at the age of thirty-one, is a widely publicized exception. Former attorney general Janet Reno has also called attention to the disease. Parkinson's is a progressively disabling disease, marked by increasing muscle tremor and stiffness. People with Parkinson's have to cope with the same poor coordination and faulty balance as is seen in MS. In addition, they frequently lose the ability to show the full range of facial expressions and exhibit the so-called Parkinson mask.

The disease occurs when neurons in the brain stem either die or lose their ability to function properly. Eventually, the higher functions of the brain—reasoning, memory, and creativity—are affected. It is now thought that exposure to heavy metals, toxic chemicals, pesticides, or other toxins in food could be a factor in the onset of Parkinson's. A variety of drugs are used to control the tremors and to slow down the progress of the disease, and new drugs are promised. Surgical techniques are also occasionally used to cut nerves to the damaged sections of the brain. Various types of brain tissue transplants are in the experimental stage.

Amyotrophic Lateral Sclerosis

Amyotrophic lateral sclerosis (ALS) is also called Lou Gehrig's disease or motor neuron disease. In this disease, specific nerve cells in the brain and spinal cord degenerate. These cells are responsible for controlling voluntary movement. The degeneration follows a predictable sequence, unlike in MS, where it's completely unpredictable. The muscles gradually weaken and waste away, leading to paralysis.

ALS usually strikes in midlife. Men are one and a half times more likely to have the disease than women. New research indicates that a virus may be responsible for ALS.

There is no cure for ALS, and the course of the disease is typically less than ten years. New drugs may prolong the life of patients. There is usually no pain and all of the functions of the cerebral cortex—reasoning, memory, intellectual curiosity, and so forth—remain intact. The physicist Stephen Hawking has had the disease for more than twenty years and still continues his research and writing.

Myasthenia Gravis

Like MS, myasthenia gravis (MG) is a chronic autoimmune neuromuscular disorder characterized by fluctuating weakness of voluntary muscle groups. As in MS, there are good days and bad days. The muscle groups most commonly involved are the ones that control eye and eyelid movements, chewing, swallowing, coughing, and facial expressions. Muscle groups that control the extremities are not often affected. Weakness of the muscles in the chest may cause difficulty in breathing.

MG is diagnosed through a complete medical and neurological evaluation, plus a blood test for specific antibodies that are usually present if someone has the disease. Treatment is similar to treatment for MS.

Chorea

Chorea is a rare disorder of the nervous system that causes uncontrollable spasmodic muscle movements, especially of the arms, legs, and face. In Huntington's chorea, which strikes people in their thirties and forties, there is a progressive loss of mental functioning due to the continuing death of brain cells. There is no cure. Sydenham's chorea, also known as St. Vitus' dance or rheumatic chorea, may appear in children (most often girls) after they've suffered rheumatic fever. Usually the patient recovers fully after a few weeks of bed rest.

Other diseases affecting the nervous system are meningitis (inflammation of the meninges of the brain), myelitis (inflammation of the spinal cord), and neuritis (inflammation of a nerve). These diseases may be caused by microorganisms, poisoning, alcoholism, or injury. They are frequently treatable and recovery is usually expected.

Many veterans of the Gulf War developed neurological problems, including the loss of the ability to concentrate, balance and coordination problems, dizziness, and chronic fatigue—all symptoms of MS. Although causes of the Gulf War syndrome are not known for certain, some researchers believe that exposure to chemical nerve agents, pesticides, and insect repellents were a factor. Veterans who have the syndrome show definite nerve cell loss in several areas of the brain. The future of the disease is unknown.

The symptoms of a brain tumor may mimic those of neurological diseases. Usually brain tumors are diagnosed through an MRI or CAT scan and are treated with chemotherapy and surgery.

A cerebral hemorrhage or stroke can cause a variety of neurological complications, such as paralysis, muscle tremor, aphasia (loss of speech), and mental confusion. This is also true of traumatic head injury. The extent of disability depends on where the brain was injured. In both cases, recovery may be full, partial, or nonexistent.

Medical Treatment for MS

There may be no cure for MS yet, but there are a variety of treatments for its symptoms. Many people with MS do well with no drug therapy at all, other than over-the-counter remedies such as anti-inflammatories. Others may need medication only occasionally, during a flare.

Medications and therapeutic regimens may be directed toward specific symptoms or toward the disease as a whole. Others are aimed at strengthening the body and promoting overall health. Many medications have serious side effects and some carry significant risks.

Treating the Symptoms

Treating the symptoms works well for many people with MS. Unless the disease progresses, they feel no need to treat the disease itself.

Bladder Problems

Medications are available to treat the different bladder problems that occasionally arise—too frequent urination or urine retention, for instance. These treatments are taken only when needed and usually have no side effects. Sometimes catheterization (mechanical emptying of the bladder) is needed. This can be done in a clinic or doctor's office or even at home—there is no need to be hospitalized.

Sexual Problems

Some people with MS experience a diminished sex drive or do not enjoy sexual activity because of physical problems. Medications and over-the-counter products are available to improve or solve these conditions.

Vision Problems

Steroids may restore vision, but frequently sight returns on its own without the need for medication. Eye patches or special prism lenses can be prescribed to correct double vision if it persists or frequently recurs.

Spasticity

Several prescription drugs are available to ease spasticity; most are muscle relaxants. Physical therapy, swimming, and stretching exercises also help.

Pain

Over-the-counter anti-inflammatory and pain-reducing drugs (aspirin, acetaminophen, and ibuprofen, for instance) can be taken for minor aches and pains. These drugs should not be overused. Medical advice is necessary for serious pain.

Muscle Weakness

Corticosteroids, often taken intravenously, can reduce inflammation and restore mobility. They seem to shorten the duration of an MS attack and may also reverse a loss of myelin. Frequently prescribed steroids include adrenocoricotropic hormone (better known as ACTH), prednisone and prenisolone, methylprednisolone, betamethasone, and dexamethasone. There is some indication that steroids may be more appropriate for people with movement problems, rather than sensory disabilities, although they are also routinely prescribed for problems with vision.

These corticosteroids differ from anabolic steroids, which are occasionally given to athletes to build muscle mass and have no therapeutic properties.

Steroids carry significant risks and the side effects may outweigh their advantages in some people. One of the most characteristic signs of using steroids is puffiness (water retention), especially a "moon face" and the accumulation of fat on the back of the neck. Overuse can lead to a loss of calcium, even the development of osteoporosis; the formation of cataracts; high blood pressure; and an impaired immune system. All these adverse side effects don't usually appear in one person. When carefully monitored, the drugs are usually safe for most people and will continue to be used for MS flare-ups.

Depression
Both depression and fatigue are common in MS and both can be treated with antidepressants plus common sense. Fatigue frequently brings on depression, so staying well-rested and pacing one's activities are important. A determination to "think positive" also helps.

Treating the Disease

Because MS is a highly individualized disease, with no two patients exactly alike, treating it is a real challenge. The drug that works beautifully for one patient will not work at all, or will have disastrous side effects, for another. For those willing to risk taking part in trials with new drugs, this is an exciting time. Pharmaceutical labs come out with new possibilities almost weekly. Other new treatments are also emerging.

Immunotherapy

The goal of using immunotherapy to treat autoimmune diseases is to reduce the immune response against normal body tissue while keeping intact the immune response to antigens. This is a complex process that must be carefully monitored.

Some immunosuppression drugs that are given to slow or inhibit the body's usual immune response are Cyclosporin, Methotrexate, and Azathioprine. The great danger in using this kind of immunotherapy is that the patient becomes vulnerable to every infection that he or she is exposed to.

Immunoglobulin therapy (IVIg) is a fairly recent treatment that has shown promising results so far. Immunoglobulin—one of the body's naturally occurring antibodies—is given intravenously once a month to patients with relapsing-remitting multiple sclerosis. It appears to reduce the frequency of relapses. There are no apparent adverse side effects. Seventeen-year-old Marybeth reports a downside: She finds the treatment frustrating and boring because she must stay still for the hours it takes to complete it.

The latest drugs to be approved for MS treatment are as simple as A B C: Avonex, Betaseron, and Copaxone. Avonex and Betaseron are synthetic forms of interferon, a naturally occurring protein that neutralizes ("interferes with") viruses. They promise to reduce the frequency and severity of relapses and even to slow the progress of the disease.

Avonex is injected intramuscularly (into the muscle) once a week; Betaseron is injected subcutaneously (under the skin) every other day.

For some patients, like twenty-three-year-old Margery, Avonex is a miracle drug. After battling MS for five years, she says her life has returned to "normal"—chasing her two-year-old son, going for long walks with her husband, having fun with friends. "No one could guess I have multiple sclerosis," she laughs. "Sometimes I even forget!"

But Sam, also twenty-three, couldn't tolerate the drug, although he tried it for several months. "I felt like I had the flu the whole time—fever, chills, nausea, exhaustion. MS never made me so sick that I had to go to bed, but Avonex did."

Betaseron is similar to Avonex both in results and side effects.

Copaxone (glatiramer acetate) is a mixture of synthetic amino acids, the same amino acids found in myelin. It may serve as a decoy for the immune system, reducing its attacks on myelin, or it may promote myelin tolerance. It apparently brings about a very specific response that doesn't involve the entire immune system. Therefore, the side effects—if any—are usually confined to a soreness and redness around the site of the injection. It, like Betaseron, is injected subcutaneously and can be done by the patient.

Early reports show that Copaxone reduces the frequency of relapses by about one-third. It also may slow the progress of the disease, cutting back on the need for steroids. At this point, Copaxone is very expensive and difficult to obtain because it takes so long to produce. In the years ahead, it will likely become more accessible.

Plasmapheresis

Plasmapheresis, the exchange of plasma, has been used to treat autoimmune and neurologic diseases for years. It has been used as a treatment for MS only recently, and it is still considered to be in the experimental phase. The early results at the Mayo Clinic in the fall of 1999 were very encouraging, but so far, the process is not widespread. It is expensive and not without risk.

During a plasma exchange, all of the patient's blood is removed, treated, and restored. This may take as long as four hours. While it is "out," the blood cells are mechanically separated from the plasma—the clear fluid component of blood. The blood cells are then mixed with replacement plasma, and the mixture is returned to the patient. The idea is that the antibodies that attack myelin will be removed and the disease will then go into remission.

While it is not clearly understood why, plasma exchange benefits some patients and not others. The dangers are many: the procedure may induce a hemorrhage or a serious allergic reaction, the fluid balance is upset during the procedure, and medications and "good" antibodies are removed along with the unwanted material. The process is extremely hard on the patient and takes days to recover from. It is usually considered only in cases of severe flares that do not respond to corticosteroids.

Therapy to Improve Nerve Impulse Conduction

Because the transmission of electrochemical messages between the brain and body is disrupted in MS, medications to improve the conduction of nerve impulses are being investigated. Demyelinated nerves show abnormal potassium levels, so scientists are experimenting with drugs that normalize nerves' potassium levels, thereby restoring conduction of nerve impulses. Several trials show improvement in symptoms.

Other experimental therapies include lymphoid irradiation, bone marrow transplant, and remyelination. None is yet widespread or especially successful. Remyelination is discussed in chapter 9.

Alternate Therapies

The enthusiasm for alternatives to traditional medicine has grown in the last few years. Some of these therapies may help with the symptoms of MS, but most do not. Still, the National Multiple Sclerosis Society thinks a few are worth investigating.

Some alternative therapies that have been long discounted are the electrical stimulation of the spinal cord, removal of the thymus gland, injections of beef heart and hog pancreas extracts, and surgical implantation of pig brain. Removal of the thymus gland, where the immune system's T cells are manufactured and stored, is still considered today for some autoimmune diseases.

Another suggestion that continues to pop up today despite negative publicity is the removal of amalgam dental fillings. These fillings are made of silver and mercury, and it is well known that mercury has a harmful effect on the nervous system. It has been thought that leakage from such fillings might be toxic. However, the amount of mercury in fillings is quite small, probably not nearly enough to cause brain damage.

Replacing fillings is expensive and stressful, entailing long stretches in the dentist's chair. It might be worth it if there were significant benefits, but so far none have been verified.

The MS Society has provided a research grant to study the possibility of treating the disease with apitherapy—injecting the venom from bees into patients. The obvious side effects are the same as being stung by bees—pain, inflammation, stiffness, soreness, and itching. In some cases there may be a more serious allergic reaction that requires prompt medical attention.

The recorded benefits of apitherapy so far have not been great, although enough people have claimed relief from MS symptoms to encourage the continuation of the investigation. The theory is that the highly inflammatory venom will trigger an outpouring of anti-inflammatory hormones that will overcome the inflammation of the myelin. There is a similar theory regarding the injection of snake venom, a far more dangerous undertaking. No one claims that either type of venom could alter the course of the disease or provide a cure.

A therapy called hyperbaric oxygen that became popular in the 1980s was intended to arrest the course of MS as well as improve its symptoms. It involved breathing pure oxygen under increased pressure in a specially constructed chamber. This therapy has generally been discredited.

Today, magnetism is advertised as a kind of cure-all. The Food and Drug Administration (FDA) takes a dim view of using magnets for pain relief, despite the endorsements by professional athletes. Magnetism is supposed to be especially beneficial for joint and muscle pain, and thousands of people claim it has helped them.

Some scientists agree there could be some value in wearing magnets. Laboratory tests were recently conducted with specially fitted magnets that are slightly stronger than those you'd use to hang a grocery list on your refrigerator. Participants in the study didn't know if they had a real magnet or a fake one, as they were labeled in code. Results showed that there was a reduction in pain for the magnetized participants and not for the unmagnetized ones.

Acupuncture can be used to relieve pain and muscle spasm, as can massage and hydrotherapy, but none of these affect the disease process.

The list of dietary supplements—vitamins, herbs, and homeopathic remedies—that MS patients claim have helped them is long. Success is usually achieved by trial and error and is idiosyncratic. There appears to be no scientific proof that megavitamin therapy favorably or unfavorably affects the course of the disease.

Several clinical trials have shown that adding polyunsaturated fatty acids (such as evening primrose oil) to the diet can slow the progression of the disease and slightly reduces the severity and duration of MS flares in some people. Some people are certain that eliminating processed food with preservatives and artificial coloring helps them.

Do people who try alternative therapies do better in the long run than those who stay with traditional medicine? It's impossible to say, but traditional medicine is more willing to look seriously at alternative therapies today than ever before.

Psychological Adjustment

When Kelly first heard her diagnosis, everything became surreal. She looked at her parents. She looked at the floor. She looked everywhere but at the doctors. She could not believe what was happening. Her ears didn't seem to be working right—the words she was hearing sounded garbled.

All she could think about was that her dreams were history. Forget the tennis team. And what good is a blind geologist in a wheelchair? What about getting married and having children? Who would take care of her? How disappointed her parents must be! She didn't want to be a burden on them. After all, they had lives of their own. Would she have to return to being a child forever? Her brain went into overdrive.

She became aware of the heavy silence in the room. Everyone was looking at her. Dr. Garfield said emphatically, "Kelly, don't write off your life. I can see by the look on your face that you're in shock. That's normal. Just know we will be taking good care of you."

Kelly told herself not to cry, but she felt tears streaming down her cheeks. She felt that her whole body was full of tears and she'd never be able to get rid of them all.

The psychological adjustment to MS can be very difficult. To be suddenly faced with a diagnosis of an unpredictable, lifelong disease is disorienting, even shattering. Questions leap out. Will I be dependent on people to live? How will I function? Will I be able to work? How will I get around? How will this disease affect me and my friends? How can I help myself? Am I good for anything?

We can "what if" until the moon looks square. It doesn't change anything, and after a while, all we do is drive ourselves crazy. Whether we want to or not, we must go through the steps of the grieving process: denial, bargaining, depression, anger, and acceptance. Only then can we allow hope to return and start to cope with the situation. There seems to be no shortcut or any chance to avoid a step. Few people go through the steps in the same order, and many repeat a step or two.

Grief

Grief, the intense sorrow triggered by the loss of someone or something dear to us, can be an overwhelming emotion. None of us wants to feel it, and we will all go to great lengths to avoid it. Usually we can't feel it all at once but must suffer through it in layers or stages. As symptoms change in MS, it's often necessary to go through the grieving process more than once.

The grief following a great loss can seem unbearable, but it is actually a healing process. We grieve the loss of a loved one, the loss of a limb, the loss of the way we want our bodies to perform, the loss of dreams, the loss of favorite activities.

For young people diagnosed with MS, one of the most severe disappointments is the loss of the chance to participate in athletics. Joe lived for basketball, Erica loved softball, and Clay was on the wrestling team. Each of these sports was a part of them, and it wasn't easy to give them up.

"I was a cross-country runner," said Tim, "with big ambitions toward the Olympics. Nothing was harder than giving up that dream. It still hurts to think of it, but I can hike when it's cool enough, as long as I rest along the way, so I try to be content with that. Maybe I'll need a cane or a walker someday, but I'll put one foot in front of the other as long as I can."

During the grief process, it is common to have many conflicting feelings. Sorrow, anger, loneliness, sadness, shame, anxiety, fear, and guilt often accompany serious losses. Having so many strong feelings can be very stressful. The urge to go back to bed and pull the covers over your head can be strong.

Denial

At first, you may deny the loss that has taken place and withdraw from your usual social contacts. Is there a better way to get rid of a problem than to deny that it even exists? This may work in the very short run, but it won't work for the rest of your life. By denying MS's existence, you tell yourself that you don't have it. But in this case, wishing won't make it so. Denial may last only a few moments, or as long as several years.

Ira Lipsky, now an outspoken advocate for people who have MS, says he was in denial for ten years. It nearly wrecked his life. He was trying so hard not to see what was obvious to everyone else that he failed to notice how unhappy his family was.

Denying your feelings and failing to allow yourself to grieve is actually harder on your mind and body than going through the pain. When people say, "Look on the bright side," or suggest other ways of cutting off difficult feelings, you may feel pressured to hide or to deny these emotions. Hiding or denying your emotions only makes it take longer for healing to occur.

Sixteen-year-old Sue knows this, but she doesn't want to make her mother more upset than she already is. "I feel like I can't show my sadness, depression, or anger," she said, "for if I do, my family and friends will worry more about me. I want to talk to someone who understands."

Someone who understands might be a doctor, teacher, minister, rabbi, or social worker, if it can't be a relative. They won't judge you, and they will allow you to express your feelings without making you feel guilty for having them.

Anger
You may be furious with the world for "letting" MS invade your body. You may even be angry with yourself for "allowing" MS into your life. Realistically, nothing could have prevented you from contracting MS. At this point, we don't have a vaccine to keep MS out of our lives.

A common question for anyone to ask when faced with a serious problem is "Why me?" The obvious answer is "Why not you?" None of us can get through life without problems, and life isn't fair. Knowing that doesn't mean you accept it. Unfairness steams most people.

Anger must be acknowledged. That is the first step in dealing with it. Pound a pillow, hit some tennis balls, howl at the moon. Doing something physical helps to release the tight feeling in your head and chest.

Then it's time to figure out what to do with the anger. Anger is a powerful emotion. Releasing it can channel your energy in a more positive direction. Some angry people become advocates for others caught up in unfair situations, whether as lawyers or politicians or volunteers for a cause. Others use it to strengthen themselves: "You say I can't do this? I'll show you!"

Sometimes anger is really fear. Facing your fears is a big part of coping with serious illness. Most of these fears can be dispelled through knowledge. Learning what to expect (even from an unpredictable disease) and discovering how others have coped with MS will help chase away most of the dragons.

Bargaining

You may want to make a bargain with the powers that be, asking "If I do this—give all my money to the poor, become a missionary, promise to never be angry again—will you take away the MS?" It sounds like a logical proposition, and almost everyone tries it, but unfortunately it doesn't work. After a while, the bargaining stage drops away.

Depression

A feeling of numbness signals depression, although anger, fear, and sadness may remain underneath. Erica didn't want to do anything but sleep after she was diagnosed. Even talking on the phone seemed too difficult, much less having real contact with people. All the projects she was interested in seemed stupid and pointless. She gave up participating in Little Theater and put away her guitar.

Depression has been compared to seeing the world in gray instead of in color or hearing only one note of a song instead of the whole melody. Life becomes narrow and small; there doesn't seem to be room for anyone or anything else.

Fatigue and depression are closely related. Sometimes interacting with people is honestly too exhausting for someone with MS. Is it depression or fatigue or both that keeps Erica homebound? A doctor is the one to make this diagnosis. Both fatigue and depression can be treated, and there is no reason to let this stage hang around too long.

A good cry will frequently loosen up the frozen feelings of depression. For those who have difficulty crying on their own, reading a sad book or renting a tearjerker can help.

Acceptance

Acceptance occurs when the anger, sadness, and mourning have tapered away. The grieving person simply accepts the reality of the loss. From the acceptance stage, the grieving person can go on with life, dealing with the loss in a constructive manner.

"Okay," said Joe. "I can't play serious basketball again. But I can play a little one-on-one or a pickup game with the guys now and then. And I can take management courses and maybe work for a pro team that way. It could be interesting. And I won't have to worry about a trick knee or retiring before I'm forty."

Hope and Coping

Hope signals the end of grieving. One day there may be a lightening of mood and a desire to look to the future with some enthusiasm. Energy returns, music plays on key, and the sun breaks through the clouds. Life seems possible again.

Coping skills come with education, experience, and practice. The first rule to remember is: Be good to yourself. Hitting yourself with a mallet because you're not progressing fast enough or because you're not ready to give up anger or sorrow completely gives you nothing but a sore head.

Grieving and its stresses pass more quickly with good self-care habits. Eat a balanced diet, watch the caffeine, get plenty of rest, do the exercises your physical therapist recommends, and take the medications prescribed by your doctor. Just knowing you're doing all you can helps you psychologically.

Most of us are unprepared for grief. Tragedy usually strikes suddenly, without warning. Practicing good self-care habits helps you deal with the pain and shock of any loss until acceptance is reached.

It also helps to have a close circle of family and friends. They want to help. Let them; it's good for everyone involved, especially you. Shutting them out is the worst thing you could do, even if seeing how healthy they are makes you bitter for a while.

You may want to consult a counselor if your grieving process takes a prolonged period of time or if your coping skills need some help. This doesn't mean you're weak or "intellectually challenged;" it means you're smart.

Consider joining a support group, one for MS specifically or one for all who suffer from chronic illness. Times

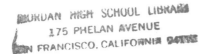
and meeting places for these groups are frequently listed in the newspaper or are available from local social service agencies. If run positively and constructively, a support group can help you through your grieving and start you on your way to acceptance. It may also introduce you to new friends.

Dozens of support groups are available on-line as well, and some of them are exclusively for those under twenty-five.

Faith

A religious faith is a powerful coping tool for many people. Following the rituals of the seasons in a temple, mosque, or church with like-minded people can bring a sense of peace to even the most troubled mind. Participation in the religious life often offers stability and reassurance.

Humor

Humor is the best medicine. It certainly is the easiest to take. Even doctors are coming around to that point of view. Many psychotherapists find humor invaluable in helping their clients release emotions surrounding the death of a loved one or a significant loss in their lives.

While we know laughing makes us feel better emotionally, scientists have found that it actually improves physical health by decreasing tension (and therefore pain) and increasing circulation—that's where the warm feeling laughing brings about comes from. Another result is accelerated breathing and sharpened brain function. In other words, jokes—even dumb ones—make us smarter.

Laughter immediately puts things in perspective. It breaks the ice of frosty relationships and softens racial, cultural, and religious differences. It can also help you through embarrassment and frustration and is a sure, instant cure for self-pity.

The first time MS sufferer Roger wet his pants in public, he was mortified. It was in an upscale department store in a mall. "They'd hidden their rest room," he recalled. "I stopped at the jewelry counter to ask where it was when whoops! I backed out of there so fast you would have thought I was on wheels. I really thought I'd die from the embarrassment. But that night I woke up at about 2 AM and started to laugh. What a hoot! You should have seen the look on that woman's face! I really made her day!"

Whether you respond to pie-in-the-face slapstick or sophisticated comedy, humor is a great healer. You can log on to http://www.cripworld.com on the Web for humor by and for the disabled.

Choices

Everyone has choices all the way through life. For instance, as Kelly's diagnosis begins to sink in, she can choose to be positive or negative about it. Of course no one can be positive twenty-four hours a day, seven days a week, but we can either have a positive outlook or see the world through smudged glasses.

Let's say Kelly did not grieve about having MS and the losses she saw in her future. When presented with the opportunity to work through the stages of the grieving process, she turned her face to the wall. She became angry and bitter, alienating both her family and friends. Eventually she isolated herself from the people and activities she once enjoyed. Now, the once vivacious and active Kelly spends most of her time watching television by herself.

This isn't living; it's just marking time.

Complaining may be a way to get negative feelings off your chest, but it may also become a habit. Seventeen-year-old Teresa struggles with "the curse of MS," complaining about everything. "When my friends call, I have to tell them I can't go anywhere because I have a headache. I hate headaches. My medicine tastes awful—sometimes I can barely swallow it. I miss too much school and I've gotten behind in everything." Teresa might change her attitude or might be even more of a grumbler forty years hence. If so, she'll probably have an audience of one.

On the other hand, say that Kelly worked hard to get through the pain of knowing she had MS and realizing the possible losses she might encounter. She cried, she raged, she asked for help when she needed it. She went through about six months of emotional turmoil before becoming ready to put energy back in her life.

Finally she was willing to accept the facts and adjust to the losses. Because of her concern for others facing the disease, she decided to become active in the local MS chapter as a peer counselor. Offering her time and talents to benefit the organization gave Kelly a boost to her sense of self-esteem. In her own way, and according to her own timetable, she worked through the stages of grief and made lemonade out of lemons.

Grieving is a way of releasing and letting go of the past in order to participate fully in the present with anticipation of the future.

What to Expect from Other People

The people around us are as varied as we are. They have the same complex set of feelings, aspirations, and frustrations. Their responses to your diagnosis of MS may surprise you—or it may be just what you expected.

When the question "How do your friends react to your disease?" was asked at a support group for teenagers with MS, these were some of the answers:

"I found out who my real friends were—the hard way. I learned that one of my 'friends' was saying behind my back that I was faking the symptoms just to get sympathy."

"Some of the guys I hang out with stayed away from me because they thought MS was contagious. They wouldn't even touch the books I used! That went on until the school counselor sat them down and told them the truth. Now they're pretty much okay about everything."

"I was worried about how my friends would react to my fatigue, which started a couple of months ago. I used to be the biggest partier at my college. Now I'm ready to go to bed by ten, nine some nights. I just can't keep up with them anymore. So far, most of them have stood by me, but they hope I get well soon. They don't seem to understand what 'chronic' means."

"I know all too well about fatigue causing problems with a social life and about people not understanding. My boyfriend doesn't understand either, although he pretends to. I've found that the only way to deal with this is to not stress out over other people's opinions."

"I get discouraged when people say to me that I don't look like I'm sick because that makes me wonder if they think this is a pretend disease."

"I hate the way other people treat me—not my friends, they're great—just because I use a cane. They act like I'm deaf and retarded, as well as a gimp. They whisper to each other about me and think I don't notice."

"Everybody at my school, well, almost everybody, got cool with my MS as soon as they realized I wasn't going to conk out and die on them."

"My best friend was relieved to hear the diagnosis. She thought that because I started walking funny I was a secret drinker!"

No matter what your situation, you're going to encounter all sorts of people in life. When you have a disease that can have debilitating symptoms, like MS, these "close encounters" can be anything but ordinary. For a while, until you sort out your feelings, any encounter may be stressful.

Those Close to You

Close relationships may be a source of strength or of conflict. Sometimes a friend, sister, brother, spouse, or even parent may not be able to deal with their own feelings about your disease, much less the emotions you're experiencing. We like to think these people are rock solid and devoted to our welfare, but the truth is they're upset and confused. It may feel as if they've abandoned you and in a sense they have, but you'll have to let them go. They'll probably be back before long.

Just as you must go through a grieving process, those close to you must also grieve. Perhaps your mother is so confused about your situation that she says something that's totally off the wall. This isn't the time to hold her accountable. Perhaps your father says, "Impossible! We'll get another opinion! Your doctor is a quack." Let him yell; he'll come back to earth soon. A boyfriend or a girlfriend may think, "I don't want to be tied to an invalid." If that's his or her attitude, it's time to say good-bye, even though that means more hurt to contend with.

For those around you to adjust successfully to your MS, they must feel they can engage in open and honest communication. It's sometimes hard for people to express their feelings and needs in any situation. MS, or any disease, can complicate the situation. Your family's style may be to keep a stiff upper lip and say nothing. Or you may feel the need to protect a family member from the truth. Some relatives or friends may view their own needs as less important than yours and deny their feelings of guilt, anger, and embarrassment. Before long, they'll be wearing a martyr's expression and filling up with resentment.

As soon as you feel able, encourage openness and welcome questions. This is important to keep in mind: At your core, you are the same person after getting MS as you were before getting MS. Yes, certain physical aspects may be different, and you might have a whole new perspective on life. But the essence of you remains unchanged. People must understand that and so must you.

Part two of that statement is that the people around you are the same, too. No one is automatically changed into a saint. Irritations will still be irritating and family dissension will still occur. If your big brother teased you before you got sick, he'll stop for a while, but he'll start up again. You may be a celebrity for a few weeks, but eventually you'll have to hang up your clothes, do the dishes, and take out the trash just like you used to.

If you are married, there is no doubt that MS will put a strain on the marriage, both financially and emotionally. But it can be worked through if both partners are willing to be honest with themselves and each other—and to keep in mind why you got married in the first place. Many MS couples not only weather the storm, but come through it stronger than ever.

The Kindness of Strangers

You may feel self-conscious in public and wonder what other people think of you. If you have to use some assistive device to get around, such as a cane, walker, wheelchair, or scooter, you may feel that all eyes are on you. You may even feel inferior, a less than adequate person.

Most of the time, people genuinely want to be helpful, friendly, and understanding. They don't judge you harshly when something out of your control is making life more challenging than usual.

Think back to the time before you got MS. Didn't you want to provide assistance to someone who needed it, whether you knew the person or not? You didn't pass judgment and it wasn't a big deal. This isn't to say that you must encourage others to help you all the time. You

will lose your independence if you do. Time and experience will help you know when to accept help willingly
and to realize that no one thinks less of you for needing
assistance now and then. Most people respect a person
who tries to achieve a goal despite some kind of personal
challenge, even if that goal is just to walk forty feet from
a car to the door of a restaurant. Don't you?

And your friends and family won't care how you get
somewhere or how long it takes you as long as you get
there and they can see you.

Different Reactions

One veteran of the MS war has found there are basically
four categories of people in regard to the disabled: the
Truly Helpful, the Overly Helpful, the Sympathizers, and
the Stunned. Family members, friends, coworkers,
acquaintances, and strangers can be any one of the four
and people can move from one category to another. For
instance, a Sympathizer can become one of the Truly
Helpful with the right motivation and the right education.

Beware of the Overly Helpful, though. They are really a
form of Sympathizer and not Truly Helpful. They may want
to protect you from life or they may be trying for the Nurse
of the Year Award. Whatever their motivation, they'll get in
the way of your goal to be as self-sufficient as possible.

The Truly Helpful are a godsend. They give without
judging and sometimes provide help almost telepathi-
cally. Truly Helpful people see a person who could have
an easier time if they provided a little assistance and
instinctively do the right thing. This help may come in

the form of lending a hand with housework or yard work, helping someone move through a tricky passage, or simply opening a door. You will be surprised at the kind and selfless acts that can come from people. Cherish these people, honor their efforts to help, and express your thanks.

The Sympathizers are usually helpful, but not as much as the Truly Helpful. Sympathizers typically act out of pity, guilt, or a lack of understanding of what is really needed. Oftentimes, Sympathizers won't make situations easy for you, although they act as if they want to. When you're struggling to walk or to pick up something that's fallen on the floor, the last thing you want or need is for someone to rush over and tell you, "Bless your heart, I know it must be tough. I'm so sorry for you." That's not motivating. It's frustrating.

Wouldn't it be more inspiring to hear, "Good for you! You stuck it out and made it all the way from the car! Is there anything I can help you with?" When the offer is genuine, it's easy to say, "Sure. Would you put this package in the backseat for me?"

With time and perhaps a tactful suggestion or two, a Sympathizer can become Truly Helpful.

Then there are the Stunned. Stunned people are caught off guard by seeing someone who's out of the ordinary. They either stare at a disabled person or act as if such a person is invisible. They do so for a variety of reasons: ignorance, lack of training in good manners, or curiosity—rarely meanness. If you work the experience right, you will not only turn these people into helpers but may even get a laugh from their behavior.

Have you ever watched people who are trying not to look at someone or something? Their eyes move hither and thither as they struggle to keep their head facing straight ahead. Sometimes they even run into someone else, or the wall, while they're busy pretending not to look.

Children are frequently among the Stunned, but at least they are honest about it. "Why do you walk funny, Mister?" is a straightforward question that is easy to answer. Consider that answering such questions is an important part of a child's education. Perhaps you are setting that child on the path of being Truly Helpful.

The use of mechanical devices usually turns heads. If you use a lift to load or unload a wheelchair or a scooter, expect people to look. Some have never seen this operation before. The mechanically inclined want to learn how everything works. The uncomfortable walk by as though the whole assembly and process is invisible; they may secretly be afraid they will someday be using similar equipment or they just may want to deny the presence of illness and disability, hoping that will make it go away. And some people will walk up and ask you about the hardware, how it works, who provides it, and how much it costs. These people may know someone in a similar situation or anticipate facing one themselves.

Disability Rights

Education is one of the key objectives of the disability rights movement (or "crip power"). Over the past fifteen years, the often-stereotypical image of the disabled, or "differently abled," has evolved from the passive, stay-at-home "victim," to the vigorous, ambitious activist who won't take "You can't!" for an answer.

The rallying cry for disability rights has been "No pity!" and their marches and demonstrations have called attention to problems of accessibility and full participation in the life of a community, including the same rights to transportation, accommodations, and communications that "abled" people enjoy.

Brian, a nineteen-year-old with MS, organized a Disability Awareness Day at his junior college. Participants were assigned a walker, wheelchair, or cane or had their arms held down by weights. Some were given glasses smeared with Vaseline or earplugs to block out sound. Then they were told to try to make their way around the campus, including the rest rooms. The experience changed perceptions in a hurry, and now a study group is considering how to make facilities more accessible to all students.

One of the inspirations to the disability movement has been Zoe Koplowitz, who advocates "turtle power." She was named the National MS Society's Athlete of the Year in 1997 because she set a record for being the world's slowest marathon runner.

In 1998 she was the first person with her level of disability to compete in the Boston Marathon. It took her more than thirty hours to finish the course, and when she did she was greeted with cheers. She was disqualified from receiving a finishing medal but was flooded with medals from other runners who admired her courage. For the past several years, Zoe has led a group of runners called the Marathon Strides to raise funds for MS research—about $2 million so far.

Try a Little Positive Communication

The best way to achieve goals like accessibility, to enhance good relationships, and to improve poor relationships is through effective communication. For instance, many wonder if MS is a communicable disease. You can assure them that MS is not communicable from one person to another in any way, nor does it come from tainted food or insect bites. Spreading accurate information about MS and all chronic diseases and disabilities can only make life better for everyone.

How do you communicate effectively with other people? Here are some ideas.

Eight Steps Toward Productive Communication

1. Make communication a priority.

2. Set aside time to talk.

3. Encourage everyone to talk.

4. Respect everyone's opinion.

5. Actively listen.

6. Give everyone permission to discuss negative, as well as positive, feelings.

7. Work toward a solution, but also try to learn something from the process of finding a solution.

8. Remember that communication is ongoing, and when practiced regularly, it gets easier over time.

People will be a source of comfort, help, humor, and, yes, frustration. As you move down the road of accepting MS, your skill at dealing with people will improve if you are patient and persistent. You'll find the efforts result in rewards for everyone involved.

What You Can Do for Yourself

Although medicine holds the key to the treatment of MS and its eventual cure, people with MS can do many things to help themselves. The most important one costs nothing.

Keep a Positive Attitude

Attitude is probably the most essential part of your arsenal in the fight against MS. In fact, attitude may be the only thing over which you have control. Your attitude is extremely important! It can literally make the difference between a marginal day and a good day. You may be skeptical, but it's true. Positive thoughts may not send MS away, but they will affect you physically and psychologically.

Laura says, "I keep telling everyone that I'll be fine because I really believe that I will be. I think a big part of being well is believing that you can be and will be."

Some days the thought of a positive attitude is hard to stomach. You can do it if you push yourself a little and remember that having a positive attitude in the past has produced better days.

Limit Self-Pity

There is no need to give up self-pity totally at first, but ration it. Self-pity won't help you develop a positive self-image or lead to a positive attitude. You can see this if you write down your negative thoughts. Read them out loud and then ask yourself how they could possibly help. If you're thinking "they can't," then you're right. Of course they can't help you.

Take steps to be aware when self-pity is rearing its head. Sometimes it sneaks up on you. It is only natural to feel sad if and when your symptoms change or get worse. But work to keep your self-pity to a minimum. With experience, you'll see how counterproductive it can be and why it's necessary to stop it before it takes on a life of its own and becomes a habit that's hard to break.

Melanie's family encouraged her to feel sorry for herself, so she did—twenty-four hours a day. She thought her friends were insensitive because they wouldn't stay around to listen to her daily recitals of everything that had gone wrong or could go wrong. One day someone put a note in one of her books: "I felt sorry because I had no shoes until I saw the man who had no feet." She got the message and started to change her outlook.

Turn to Humor

Humor can get you through the tough times and make the good times even better. Try not to take yourself too seriously. When you take a tumble or do something a little klutzy (whether or not MS is involved), laugh about it. Picture it from the outside, as if you were watching a videotape of yourself, and you meant to be a clown. You might even rival Jim Carrey! Rent funny movies (the Marx Brothers, the Three Stooges), read humor, go to comedy clubs, surround yourself with people who love to laugh.

For inspiration, read *Anatomy of an Illness* to find out how humor heals. The author, Norman Cousins, literally laughed himself out of a serious illness.

Do What You Normally Do

Keep participating in the activities that bring you enjoyment. Just because you have MS doesn't mean you have to give up pleasure or become a martyr. You will still be able to do many things for fun. Make these enjoyable activities "nonnegotiable." Promise yourself you'll do them every day or so many times a week, period.

Do you like to go to lunch or dinner with family members or certain friends? Do it! Do you like listening to music or playing an instrument or both? Do it! Do you like to attend movies, concerts, or sporting events? Do it! Do you enjoy playing sports that match your abilities? Do it!

Investigate new hobbies and interests. There is a limitless number of them, from collecting (Mickey Mouse watches, porcelain pigs, WWF cards) to creating a model railroad world; from writing a screenplay to starting your own aquarium; from abstract art to zoology; from . . . But you get the picture.

Do things that make you happy. You will have a better quality of life and so will the people around you.

Reach Out to Others

It's true what is said about helping others—oftentimes you forget about your own troubles. Once you have accepted the fact that you or someone you love has MS, reach out to those who are newly diagnosed with it. Assure them that life continues with MS and what may seem to be impossible to cope with is quite possible. Convincing others will help you believe, too.

When the actress Annette Funicello was diagnosed with MS, she had to give up her career as a dancer and singer. After a period of inactivity, she found another way to use her talent and created the foundation for neurological disorders that bears her name. Olympic medalist and skier Jimmie Heuga established the Heuga Center for people with MS after his diagnosis. His traveling Snow Express show entertains crowds and raises money for the center.

David found that his frustrations about his limitations were eased when he helped out at the local Independent Living House working with severely retarded adults. Polly found that stocking shelves at the food bank made her feel useful, and Harold tutored fourth graders after school. Brian channeled his anger into the disability rights movement; Sarah put together a puppet show featuring Disabled Dog, which gave children pointers on etiquette toward the disabled.

There are countless ways to reach out to people. You can also reach out to animals. Volunteer at the Humane Society, the animal shelter, or the zoo. Even plants need attention— check with your local botanical society to find out more.

Watch Your Diet

Much has been written and said about diet and MS and the issue is somewhat controversial, with no clear guidelines to follow. One diet advocates no red meat, but allows chicken and fish. Vegetarians recommend no meat at all and say they feel great. There are reams of material available on the subject of healthy eating and so-called miracle foods.

Ask your physician what diet, if any, he or she recommends. Most advocate one that's well balanced, with no extremes in any direction. You may wish to follow certain plans on your own if it makes you feel better. Such dietary adjustments can include avoidance of high-fat food (especially fast food) or avoidance of processed food containing preservatives and additives. Read labels so you know what you're eating and can make an intelligent decision. Some people buy only organic fruits and vegetables to avoid pesticides and herbicides. These measures may help you stay healthy in general, but may or may not address MS specifically.

Avoid Alcohol, Harmful Drugs, and Tobacco

Harmful drugs and tobacco are not good for anyone, healthy or not. Don't do drugs and don't smoke; it's that simple. Research has shown that one drink of wine or beer each day may provide long-term benefits to adults. Excessive drinking, however, is never healthy.

Exercise

Find an exercise program that is good for you. Look for exercises that stretch your muscles, reduce spasticity, increase flexibility, and maintain strength. Don't exercise to the point of fatigue, only to the point of feeling good. Your physician, a physical therapist, or a personal trainer can help you find the exercise program that is best for you. Make sure these professionals are certified in their fields and are familiar with multiple sclerosis. An unqualified trainer could do more damage than good.

Some examples of beneficial exercise programs include yoga, swimming and aquatherapy, light weight-training, and floor exercises. Also consider using a competent massage therapist, one experienced in working with neuromuscular diseases. Massage could quickly become one of the entries on your "enjoyable activities" list.

John recommends movement exercises, such as Feldenkrais (used by actors and dancers) and shiatsu. "Feldenkrais improves my balance," he says. "Modified ballet lessons might help, too."

Reduce Stress

You probably can't control the amount of stress in your life, but you can control your reaction to it. Managing stress is a key to managing MS and also to enjoying life.

Keeping a sense of humor, finding enjoyable activities, and exercising regularly are all great stress busters. Specific stress reduction techniques such as biofeedback, yoga, meditation, counseling, and group therapy are also available.

The National MS Society suggests giving yourself more time to accomplish tasks and avoiding doing more than one thing at a time. Slow and easy does it. In a family or school crisis, give yourself a "time out" and watch the clouds pass or your fish swim in their tank. If you're highly stressed, you can't add anything productive to the situation anyway.

Rest

It's no secret that everyone needs rest, and people with MS particularly need rest. So get plenty. How much, you ask? Start with eight hours of sleep each night. You may need more or less sleep, depending on your body. Take a short nap or two during the day if you feel your strength or stamina waning. You can also sit down and close your eyes, listen to music, or call someone with whom you like to talk. Most of all, don't push it.

Plan your excursions so you can rest along the way. That will help ensure that you'll have a good time. If you are somewhere where a lot of walking is required (the mall, an air show, an amusement park), then break up your activity into manageable bits. Walk a little, sit and rest a little. Bring water to drink and don't let yourself get overheated. Most of all, listen to your body. It's trying to help.

Managing Specific Symptoms

Bladder Problems

Drink at least eight glasses of fluid each day. Withholding liquids is not a good idea, even though heading for the rest room every twenty minutes is a hassle. Without lots of liquid, urine will be more concentrated and more likely to irritate the bladder. Cranberry juice seems to help prevent or stop urinary tract infections. Avoid caffeinated beverages, which irritate the bladder.

Vision Problems

Use a magnifier to help you read. Use sunglasses outdoors, especially when there's a glare from snow or water.

Memory, Loss of Concentration, Poor Judgment, Impaired Reasoning

Keep to-do lists and address books up to date. Writing in a diary each night will clarify what's going on in your life and you can check it later to jog your memory. Did Joe tell you he'd go to the game with you next week? If you write it down on the calendar, you'll be sure. If you lose concentration while working, take a break and do something completely different until your mind feels rested and ready to work again.

The number one rule for everyone, whether or not they have MS, is: Don't make important decisions when you're tired, hungry, or feeling confused. No one's judgment is to be trusted under those conditions.

Mobility

A cane, walker, wheelchair, or electric scooter can become a welcome extension of yourself. Investigate lifts that will pick up a wheelchair or a scooter and move it in and out of your vehicle. Your health insurance company, state rehabilitation agency, or a federal agency or program may purchase these aids for you if you have a prescription from your neurologist, rehabilitation doctor, or other physician. Don't let the red tape get in your way. Persevere until you prevail!

Another device that may come in handy is hand controls for your vehicle. Hand controls can help you retain your independence and allow you to drive for a long time. Consider getting handicapped license plates. You may be averse to advertising your condition, but being able to use handicapped zones for parking is convenient, and sometimes necessary. Most of the time, all your physician has to do is fill out a form for the local government stating you require these license plates and they're yours. You don't have to always park in handicapped zones, but why not take advantage of them on a bad day or on a hot day? That way you can save your strength for other things—like shopping.

Aid dogs are available in some places to help you get around. They are trained to pick up dropped objects, open and close doors, pull wheelchairs, and—if necessary—scare off a potential attacker.

Other Help

The number of products for the "physically challenged" has proliferated in the past few years. Cooling suits can help keep your temperature down. Automatic injectors will help you give yourself shots. Chair lifts will help you stand up from a sitting position. Kitchen utensils with large handles, originally engineered for people with arthritis, can make kitchen chores easier. An occupational therapist can help you decide which aids are the best for you. (And check out Abledata in the Where to Go for Help section at the back of this book.)

Explore anything and everything that will make your life easier. Use your creativity—if what you need hasn't been invented yet, invent it.

Discuss your needs with one of the MS organizations listed in the Where to Go for Help section of this book. Call your local, state, and national government officials for ideas and help. This is what we pay them for—to help us when we need it.

Most of all, be good to yourself, and get as much as possible from life!

The Long-Term Outlook

Multiple sclerosis is a long-term disease. It requires thought and planning, not just for tomorrow, but for the rest of one's life. This can be daunting, but it can also be rewarding. Until about ten years ago, people with MS could expect a life full of bed rest and few opportunities to socialize. Today, the attitude is "Reach for the sky," which can even mean hang gliding or bungee jumping.

MS patient advocate Ira Lipsky writes, "Today, MS families can go anywhere and do almost anything. From white-water rafting, hot air ballooning, and camping in Yellowstone to watching the constellations and listening to the lapping of waves on Maine granite or Hawaiian black sand."

But before any of these great projects are undertaken, they need thought and planning. For instance, want to go to Busch Stadium in St. Louis to watch Mark McGwire hit another home run? You'll need to plan how to maneuver the journey from the parking lot to the stadium, how to handle the stairs (is there a lift or elevator? ramps?), how to reserve a seat in the shade, scope out where the rest rooms are before you need one, bring a cushion for those hard stadium seats, and know when it's time to leave—even if it's only the sixth inning. These are all common sense procedures that take a little time but will ensure that you'll have a great time at the game. Information on locating specific how-to information about traveling is found in the Where to Go for Help section of this book.

Now, what about larger issues?

Family

Can I Think About Marriage?

Sure, why not? Marriage is an important part of life and there's no reason why you shouldn't enjoy it as much as anyone else. If you already had a serious boyfriend or girlfriend before diagnosis, it is very important that you talk about the effect of your disability frankly—maybe even visit the doctor together—and get all of your reservations out into the open. If your friend seems skittish, listen to his or her fears and acknowledge them. It may be that the person you love and want to spend the rest of your life with is not able or willing to risk a marriage to you. That hurts, but it's much better to learn that now, rather than two years after the "I do's" have been said.

What About Having a Baby?

This requires even more thought than marriage. You're going to marry an adult, who presumably can stick a dinner in the microwave and run a washing machine when necessary. But a baby requires full-time, active care for at least three years. The chance that you'll feel up to child care for every day of those three years is not 100 percent, so think of alternatives: Will your spouse or partner be able to stay home now and then to help out? Is there a relative who could pitch in? Neighbors or friends who could be on call? A drop-in day care center nearby?

Studies show that pregnancy—or the hormones that circulate in your system during pregnancy—frequently causes MS to go into remission. That's the good news. Studies also show that after delivery, there's often a phase of exhaustion, when your body wants to rest and recover. Sometimes postpartum depression can be severe and your worst MS symptoms appear and linger longer than usual.

It is wise to get all the information you can from your doctor or midwife before deciding to risk pregnancy. How important is having a child? Only you and your spouse or partner can answer that question.

Home Management

Managing your home, unless you're compulsively neat, probably won't be a problem except when there's a flare and that's when maid services or homemaking services can be called upon. Yard work during the summer months may be too much to attempt alone. Can you afford to hire someone or would it be easier to give up on having a garden?

When it's time to go house hunting, bring a checklist. A one-level house would be best and a large bathroom with space to maneuver is ideal. Where will the laundry facilities be? Preferably not in the basement. Measure doorways and entryways. You may never be in a wheelchair or scooter, but a friend or relative might be. Before you make a large investment, try to think of every eventuality, including transportation needs and weather conditions. (Long icy sidewalks are treacherous; a bedroom with a southern exposure might be a nightmare in the summer.)

Work

Can I Plan a Career?

Emphatically, yes. Just be realistic about what you choose to do and how much training is involved. Talk to career counselors and people in your chosen field to get a clear idea of the requirements and the responsibilities that you will encounter.

Long-range economic planners predict that the average person starting out in the workforce today will have to change jobs or careers several times to keep up with technology and trends in the marketplace. No longer do people choose a job or career and hold on to it for fifty years. Flexibility is the watchword of the future, whether in flextime, telecommuting, shared jobs, or new arrangements that are still on the drawing board.

Flexibility suits disabled workers just fine and, in fact, presents them with opportunities to achieve more than ever before. Work is an integral part of our lives and money is only part of the reason we work. The chance to use our creativity, to be part of a team, to make a contribution to others, to bring about change, to participate fully in life—these are all reasons we want to work.

The National Multiple Sclerosis Society believes that, given the right situation, almost everyone with MS can be working in a productive, fulfilling job. The "right situation" is available more often today because of the Americans with Disabilities Act (ADA), which was passed in 1990.

The ADA prohibits private employers with fifteen or more employees from discriminating against otherwise-qualified people with disabilities. Disability is defined as "a physical or mental impairment that substantially limits one or more major life activities." These activities include walking, seeing, hearing, and performing tasks that involve use of the hands. "Otherwise-qualified" means someone who meets the job's requirements for skill, experience, and education.

The law also states that if such a person is hired, reasonable accommodation must be made to compensate for the disability. Architectural barriers are now illegal. Work environments are being altered—ramps installed, bathrooms modified, electronic doors built. Since people with MS are unusually heat-sensitive, the installation of air-conditioning, if not already present, can be called a reasonable accommodation. Instead of working steadily for eight hours, it may be more effective for someone with MS to take a thirty-minute break every two hours, or even a siesta after lunch, and stretch out the workday.

In order to get any accommodations in the workplace, it will be necessary to disclose your condition. Disclosure is a very sensitive and controversial issue today. Legally, you don't need to discuss your medical history with your employer any more than you need to discuss your family life. If you anticipate problems, it might be better to explain the situation while you're well than to wait for a crisis.

Sometimes admitting to a disability will cause tension. Your coworkers might resent it if you get special treatment. They have problems, too, after all. Using your communication skills, good humor, and good attitude will help keep the situation friendly.

What If I Get Sick?

A major dilemma that people with MS face is the unpredictability of flares. Not only do you not know when they will strike, you don't know how long they will last, how severe they will be, or where they'll settle in—your eyes? bladder? mobility? Or will it be a debilitating fatigue that keeps you bed-bound?

Another piece of federal legislation can help here: the Family and Medical Leave Act (FMLA). FMLA requires that an employer allow employees twelve weeks of unpaid leave per year because of a serious health condition of their own or of a family member or due to a new child in the family. When the employee returns to work, he or she must be given the old position (or one comparable), with the same pay and benefits. During the time the employee is on leave, health insurance coverage must be continued by the employer. No one can be fired for being sick for four months. If the illness stretches beyond that time—which it rarely does with MS, particularly with today's treatments—there may be problems in keeping the job.

What If I'm Disabled by MS?

Fortunately, there are several types of disability insurance plans that are available. Private insurance is generally excellent, but very expensive. Company policies usually require that you work for them for a certain number of years before they go into effect. Some allow you to retire at full pay; others give you a pittance. Social Security Disability Insurance (SSDI) will provide income if you meet the requirements. "Disabled" to the Social Security

Administration means that you have an impairment significant enough to "preclude your engaging in substantial gainful activity of a type that exists in the national economy." This is not always easy to prove and can take a long time. Don't count on instant benefits. You should investigate all of these programs, even if you feel great and are confident you will be working all your life.

The Future of MS

The 1990s were proclaimed the Decade of the Brain, and funds for research for all neurological disorders increased. More advances were made in the neurological sciences in that decade than in the preceding fifty years. Add those advances to the continued intense research in immunology, plus the search for breakthrough drugs, and the next ten years look just as exciting.

Some examples:

➥ Scientists at the University of Illinois Biotechnology Center are experimenting with the genetic engineering of T cells, which seem to go haywire in autoimmune diseases. They want to figure out how to improve the way T cells recognize antigens. It is possible they can "learn" not to attack myelin or anything else that belongs in the body. If so, this would be a major step forward in ending autoimmune disease.

➥ At Washington University's School of Medicine, microbiologists have identified a protein that, when injected into laboratory animals, causes MS symptoms. If this peptide can be proved to be a factor in human MS, a drug can be developed to hold it in check.

☞At Cornell University Medical College, scientists have isolated myelin-making cells in the brain that may be stimulated to replace damaged myelin and possibly restore nerve function. The cells may also be implanted from healthy tissue. This procedure is called remyelination.

The special impetus behind the drive for effective, affordable remyelination is the Myelin Project, an international effort coordinated by Augusto Odone and his late wife Michaela Odone, whose story was dramatized in the 1992 movie *Lorenzo's Oil*. All the research that they fund is directed toward problem-solving and patient benefit.

Three major strategies of the project are the coordination of researchers' work, interaction between researchers and laypeople, and the prompt financing of practical experiments without red tape. The coordination is important because it allows scientists in France, for instance, to build on work that is being done in Wisconsin.

Kelly may see a cure for MS in her lifetime.

Glossary

antigen A substance that stimulates the production of an antibody.

ataxia Poor muscle coordination.

autoimmune disease A process in which the body's immune system causes illness by attacking parts of the body that are essential for health.

B cells White blood cells responsible for humoral immune responses, used to fight bacterial infections.

blood-brain barrier A membrane that controls the passage of substances from the blood into the central nervous system and normally prevents damaging or dangerous elements from reaching the brain.

central nervous system (CNS) Brain, brain stem, and spinal cord.

chronic Long lasting, always present.

cytokines Biochemicals produced by the immune system, which may be involved in autoimmune diseases.

demyelination Damage caused to the myelin sheath by recurrent attacks of inflammation; results in scars called plaques, which interrupt communications between the nerves and the rest of the body.

evoked potential test A painless diagnostic test that records electrical changes in the brain in response to repeated electrical shocks applied to a peripheral nerve; the test can confirm the presence of a suspected lesion not shown by an MRI scan.

gray matter Portions of the central nervous system where nerve cell bodies are concentrated.

immunity Security against any particular disease or poison.

immunoglobulin Proteins that function as antibodies in the immune response.

immunosuppression Any form of treatment or drug that slows or inhibits the body's usual immune responses.

interferons Antiviral proteins that affect the immune system.

lymphocytes Cells formed in lymphoid tissue that function in the development of immunity.

macrophage A scavenger cell that destroys invading antigens.

MRI Magnetic resonance imaging; produces electronic images of the inside of the body.

myelin A fatty covering that insulates nerve cell fibers in the brain.

myoclonus Irregular involuntary contraction of muscles.

oligodendroglia Collected cells in the central nervous system that produce the myelin sheath.

optic neuritis Inflammation of the optic nerve that causes transient or permanent loss of vision.

paresthesia Sensation of "pins and needles" that develops with damage to a pain pathway; a spontaneously occurring sensation of burning, prickling, or creeping on the skin.

plaque A patch of demyelinated or inflamed CNS tissue.

remission The lessening or disappearance of symptoms of any chronic disease.

remyelination The process of rebuilding myelin.

Schwann cells Cells that produce myelin in the peripheral nervous system.

spasticity Involuntary muscle contractions leading to spasms and stiffness or rigidity.

T cells White blood cells responsible for cell-mediated immune responses, used to fight viral infections.

Where to Go for Help

In the United States

CLAMS
(Computer Literate Advocates for MS)
P.O. Box 786
Kingston, WA 98346
Web site: http://www.clams.org

International MS Support Foundation
9240 E. Golf Links Road #291
Tucson, AZ 85720-1340
Web site: http://www.msnews.org

Multiple Sclerosis Association of America
706 Haddonfield Road
Cherry Hill, NJ 08002
(800) 532-7667 ext. 100
Web site: http://www.msaa.com

Multiple Sclerosis Foundation, Inc.
6350 North Andrews Avenue
Fort Lauderdale, FL 33309-2130
(800) 441-7055
Web site: http://www.msfacts.org

National Multiple Sclerosis Society
733 Third Avenue, 6th Floor
New York, NY 10017
(800) FIGHT-MS (344-4867)
Web site: http://www.nmss.org

In Canada

The Canadian Way-Multiple Sclerosis International
Web site: http://www.escape.ca/~debwalt

Integrated Network of Disability Information and Education
Web site: http://indie.ca

MS Society of Canada
250 Bloor Street East, Suite 1000
Toronto, ON M4W 3P9
(416) 922-6065
Web site: http://www.mssociety.ca

Research

MS research centers conducting clinical research may offer
you a chance to be a "guinea pig."

Robert P. Lisak, M.D.
Department of Neurology
Wayne State University
4201 St. Antoine Street, 6#/UHC
Detroit, MI 48201
(313) 577-1249

A. M. Rostami, M.D., Ph.D.
Department of Neurology
University of Pennsylvania Medical Center

3400 Spruce Street
Philadelphia, PA 19104
(215) 662-6557

John N. Whitaker, M.D.
Department of Neurology
University of Alabama at Birmingham
Birmingham, AL 35294-0007
(205) 934-2402
Web site: http://www.neuro.uab.edu

Myelin Project Headquarters
2001 Pennsylvania Avenue NW, Suite 225
Washington, DC 20006-1850
(202) 452-8994
Web site: http://www.myelin.org

National Institute of Neurological Disorders and Stroke
P.O. Box 5801
Bethesda, MD 20824
(800) 352-9424
Web site: http://www.ninds.nih.gov

Government Agencies

ADA—Americans with Disabilities Act
Information line for publications, questions, and referrals:
(800) 514-0301
Web site: http://www.usdoj.gov/crt/ada/adahom1.htm

Clearinghouse on Disability Information
Office of Special Education and Rehabilitation Services
Room 3132, Switzer Building
330 C Street SW
Washington, DC 20202-2524
(202) 205-8241

Job Accommodation Network (making the
workplace accessible)
(800) 526-7234

President's Committee on Employment of People
with Disabilities
(202) 376-6200
Web site: http://www50.pcepd.gov/pcepd

Advocacy

CripWorld
P.O. Box 458
Whitefish, MT 59937
Web site: http://cripworld.com

Institute on Independent Living
Petersens Vag 2
12741 Stockholm, Sweden
Web site: http://www.independentliving.org

Travel

Access-Able Travel Source, LLC
P.O. Box 1796
Wheat Ridge, CO 80034
(303) 232-2979
Web site: http://www.access-able.com

SATH—Society for the Advancement of Travelers with Handicaps
347 Fifth Avenue, Suite 610
New York, NY 10016
(212) 447-7284
Web site: http://www.sath.org

Technological Assistance

Abledata
8630 Fenton Street, Suite 930
Silver Spring, MD 20910
(800) 227-0216
Web site: http://www.abledata.com

Other Groups

International Tremor Foundation
7046 West 105th Street
Overland Park, KS 66212-1803
(913) 341-3880
Web site: http://www.aoa.dhhs.gov/aoa/DIR/115.html

National Ataxia Foundation
2600 Fernbrook Lane, Suite 119
Minneapolis, MN 55447-4752
(763) 553-0020
Web site: http://www.ataxia.org

National Rehabilitation Information Center
1010 Wayne Avenue, Suite 800
Silver Spring, MD 20910-5633
(301) 562-2400 or (800) 346-2742
Web site: http://www.naric.com

For Further Reading

Enteen, Robert. *Health Insurance: How to Get It, Keep It, or Improve What You've Got.* New York: Demos Vermande, 1996.

Holland, Nancy J., and June Halper, eds. *Multiple Sclerosis: A Self-Care Guide to Wellness.* Washington, DC: Paralyzed Veterans of America, 1998.

Holland, Nancy J., T. Jock Murray, and Stephen C. Reingold. *Multiple Sclerosis: A Guide for the Newly Diagnosed.* New York: Demos Vermande, 1996.

Kalb, Rosalind C., ed. *Multiple Sclerosis: A Guide for Families.* New York: Demos Vermande, 1998.

———. *Multiple Sclerosis: The Questions You Have—The Answers You Need.* 2nd edition. New York: Demos Vermande, 2000.

Koplowitz, Zoe, and Mike Celizic. *The Winning Spirit: Life Lessons Learned in Last Place.* New York: Doubleday, 1997.

Kraft, George H., and Marci Catanzaro. *Living with Multiple Sclerosis: A Wellness Approach.* 2nd edition. New York: Demos Vermande, 2000.

Lechtenberg, Richard. *Multiple Sclerosis Fact Book.* Philadelphia: F. A. Davis Company, 1995

Mairs, Nancy. *Waist-High in the World: A Life Among the Nondisabled.* Boston: Beacon Press, 1996.

Mendelsohn, Steven B. *Tax Options and Strategies for People with Disabilities.* New York: Demos Vermande, 1996.

Rumrill, Phillip D., Jr. *Employment Issues and Multiple Sclerosis.* New York: Demos Vermande, 1996.

Strong, Maggie. *Mainstay: For the Well Spouse of the Chronically Ill.* Northampton, MA: Bradford Books, 1997.

Index